Believed to be one of the first photographs of police officers, this 1854 picture shows a group of Manchester Peelers wearing their distinctive top hats and frock coats.

The Victorian Policeman

Simon Dell

CONTENTS

Published by Shire Publications Ltd, Midland House,
West Way, Botley, Oxford OX2 0PH, United Kingdom.
44-02 23rd Street, Suite 219, Long Island City,
NY 11101

E-mail: shire@shirebooks.co.uk   www.shirebooks.co.uk

© 2004 Simon Dell. First published 2004; reprinted 2008
and 2010. Transferred to digital print on demand 2011.
Reprinted 2012.

A CIP catalogue record for this book is available from the
British Library.

Shire Library no. 428 • ISBN-13: 978 0 74780 591 5

Simon Dell has asserted his right under the Copyright,
Designs and Patents Act, 1988, to be identified as the
author of this book.

Printed in Great Britain by PrintOnDemand-
Worldwide.com, Peterborough, UK.

12 13 14 15 16 14 13 12 11 10 9 8 7 6 5

COVER IMAGE
A group photograph of Cornwall Constabulary officers
c.1890 outside Callington Police Station.

ACKNOWLEDGEMENTS
The cover illustration is courtesy of the Devon and
Cornwall Police Museum. Other illustrations are
acknowledged with the author's grateful thanks as follows:
the Chief Constable of the Avon and Somerset
Constabulary, page 17 (bottom); Mr Mike Baker, pages 19
(left), 20 (top left); Mr Andrew Carpenter, page 33
(centre); the Chief Constable and Police Museum of the
Devon and Cornwall Constabulary, pages 4 (bottom),
6 (top), 7 (both), 20 (bottom left and right), 21, 23, 24
(both), 25 (bottom), 26 (bottom), 34 (bottom), 35 (left),
38 (bottom); the Chief Constable of the Essex
Constabulary and the Essex Police Museum, page 37 (top);
Mr Steve Gomershall, page 28 (centre); the Chief
Constable of the Greater Manchester Police and the
Greater Manchester Police Museum, pages 1, 17 (top), 30,
32 (bottom right); the Isles of Scilly Museum, page 25
(top); the Chief Constable of the Kent Constabulary and
the Kent Police Museum, page 4 (top); the Metropolitan
Police Authority, pages 3, 6 (bottom), 8, 9 (both), 10
(both), 11 (all), 12, 13 (all), 14 (all), 15 (both), 16 (both),
17 (centre), 18 (bottom), 19 (right), 20 (top right), 22, 26
(top), 28 (top and bottom), 29 (both), 31 (both), 32 (top
two and centre), 33 (top), 34 (top), 36; Mrs Frances Peek,
page 5 (bottom); the Ripon Police Museum Trust, pages 5
(top), 18 (top); the Chief Constable of the Surrey
Constabulary, page 38 (top); Tavistock Town Museum,
page 33 (bottom); Tetbury Police Museum, pages 35
(right), 37 (bottom).

The first 'Peelers' marching out on to their respective 'beats' (small groups of streets allocated to individual officers). The early uniform of the Metropolitan Police was an eight-buttoned swallowtail coat. A 4 inch (10 cm) leather stock (reduced to 2 inches, 5 cm, in 1859) was worn inside the high collar to guard the officer against strangulation. Until 1861 white trousers were worn in the summer; they were not standard issue but were purchased by the officers themselves. The top hat was 6 inches (15 cm) tall with a 2 inch (5 cm) wide brim. It had a black leather top and inside there were stays of cane on either side.

INTRODUCTION

If a ten-year-old Princess Victoria had been standing in Whitehall on the evening of 29th September 1829, just eight years before she came to the throne, she would have witnessed something quite new in English law enforcement: a line of men dressed in tall hats and long blue coats marching out into the streets of London. These men were members of the New Police, or 'Peelers' as they were popularly called, after their founder Sir Robert Peel. Nowadays we take our police service for granted and it is hard to imagine what life would have been like without it, but until the first few years of the Victorian age things were very different. These first police officers caused quite a stir with the public when they initially appeared, as nothing like them had been seen before on the streets of London.

Throughout history people have been appointed as upholders of the law. In King Alfred's time a type of policing occurred through a court system known as the 'Folk Moot'. The first statutory mention of the word 'constable' occurs in 1252; the term is generally believed to have derived from the Latin *comes stabuli*, 'master of the horse'.

In England at this time every man, unless excused by high office or social position, was eligible for a policing role. As time went by the laws changed, until

3

Charlie Rouse was one of the last of the old watchmen. Armed with rattle, truncheon and cutlass, he stood guard outside his box in the Brixton area of London until well into the era of Peel's New Police.

Edward I passed legislation obligating each parish to appoint two constables. The next milestone in law enforcement was the Statute of Winchester of 1285. This new law required all communities to adopt the system known as 'Watch and Ward', which involved the appointment of night watchmen to stand guard at the entrance of each town and to challenge strangers coming into that town. These watchmen patrolled the streets at night carrying a lantern and cutlass. During the reign of Charles II they were known as 'Charlies', a name that stuck until the role was finally abolished over 150 years later.

During the fifteenth and much of the sixteenth century the parish constable was pre-eminent among the four principal annually elected officers of the parish, the other three being churchwarden, surveyor of the highways and overseer of the poor. Responsibility for the appointment of local parish constables fell to the notable persons of the parish who made up the Vestry Committee (so named because its meetings were held in the vestry of the local church). Those nominated still had to carry on with

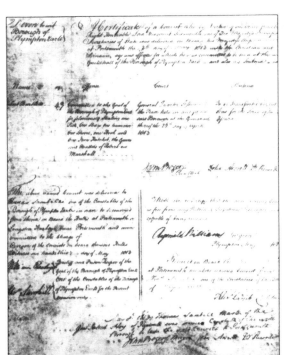

A Transportation Warrant, dated 26th April 1813, authorising the parish constable of Plympton Earle near Plymouth to take Robert Bartlett, aged forty-nine years, to Portsmouth for transportation beyond the seas. His crime was to steal one pickaxe, a sledgehammer, a shovel, a hatchet and a hook belonging to Robert Marshall. Bartlett was sentenced to seven years' transportation. This was all part of the varied duties of the parish constable at this time.

4

Constable Thomas Newton in the uniform of the North Riding Constabulary pictured in about 1856 at the time of that force's formation. Newton had previously served as the parish constable at Middleton Tyas. He retired from the service in 1871.

their own jobs and trades while serving as local officers. The role of parish constable was therefore very unpopular with men who had families to support, especially as the position did not come with any formal wages and took up much of the time that the officers could have spent making profit from their regular employment. Many men bought their way out of serving in this role.

The parish constable would take over prisoners from the watchmen and place them in the stocks or lock-up. In many instances he would keep them in his own cottage until he was able to deliver them to a Justice of the Peace. Although the parish constable wore no distinctive uniform, he was issued with a wooden truncheon, which became his symbol of authority and might have hung outside his cottage door; it also served as a defensive weapon. The truncheon was often ornately decorated, and many fine examples are still in existence.

Most parishes had about five or six parish constables, although some larger ones had more, especially during the construction of the railways – as it was at this time that drunkenness and antisocial behaviour by the railway labourers and navvies was a particular problem. The position of parish constable was held in some small towns until the eighteenth or early nineteenth century, but in

Mr Gater Potter was the last parish constable of Abbotskerswell, a village near Newton Abbot in Devon. This photograph, taken in 1857, shows him at the time of the formation of the county police force for Devon. He had been the parish constable since 1829, when Peel's 'New Police' force had been formed.

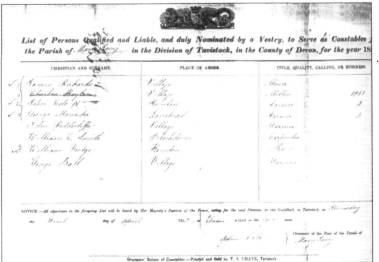

List of Persons Qualified and Liable, and duly Nominated by a Vestry, to Serve as Constables the Parish of Mary Tavy in the Division of Tavistock, in the County of Devon, for the year 18

This document is dated 1852, some four years before the formation of the local county police force. It is the list of candidates to be appointed as parish constables for the parish of Mary Tavy in west Devon. The document was completed by the Vestry Committee of the parish.

rural areas of England it lasted well into Victoria's reign, right up to the 1850s.

The overall organisation of the policing of England was in a terrible state. The watchmen were old and ineffective, the constables in the towns and cities found it impossible to maintain law and order, and decent people had to employ bodyguards to protect them at night. Highway robbers infested the roads and corruption was rife among magistrates and judges. Reform was needed and it came in the mid eighteenth century by way of the Chief Magistrate for London – Henry Fielding.

However, Fielding's reforms did not signal the end of the chaos for good; there were still problems with the system. The real turning point in the development of

the British police service was the Peterloo Massacre, which took place just after the great battle of Waterloo, before Victoria took the throne. An unlawful gathering at St Peter's Field in Manchester in 1819 was broken up by the military, which was sent in to quell the assembling masses, because there was, at that time, no police service to call upon. The outcome was that the mounted soldiers slaughtered eleven civilians and injured several hundred more. The resultant public outcry forced the government to rethink the use of the military to keep public order. This was a significant event in recognising the need

The Peterloo Massacre of 1819, St Peter's Field, Manchester.

The last recorded use of stocks in England was in 1856 in Rugby. This photograph, taken in about 1855, shows a local villain under the watchful eye of the two local police officers at Redruth in Cornwall. Judging by the grinning expression on the unfortunate criminal's face, it seems that this picture might have been set up rather than taken in earnest.

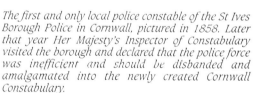

The first and only local police constable of the St Ives Borough Police in Cornwall, pictured in 1858. Later that year Her Majesty's Inspector of Constabulary visited the borough and declared that the police force was inefficient and should be disbanded and amalgamated into the newly created Cornwall Constabulary.

for a civilian police force that did not wear military-style uniforms.

As the nineteenth century progressed, growing discontent at the manner in which the country was policed, particularly in the towns and cities, created the need for reform. The system that had existed for hundreds of years could no longer cope and was slowly crumbling. Many small borough police forces, which often consisted of just one or two constables, were phased out with the creation of new county forces, the former being amalgamated into the latter. Usually the local officers simply remained in their boroughs and continued to serve under the control of the county constabularies. Many parishes, however, remained pleased with the continued efforts of their parochially appointed lawmen and so they managed to survive a little longer before the inevitable amalgamation took place.

7

THE 'BOW STREET RUNNERS'

Henry Fielding (1707–54) was well respected and known to dispense fair justice. He also made a real effort to prevent crime by encouraging the public in London to report law-breaking and to give descriptions of the criminals. In 1753 he enlisted some assistance and trained six constables who were honest men and could be relied upon to do their duty in a proper manner. These men had served their time as parish constables and so knew a little about the job already. These constables arrested so many criminals and were so successful in their work that Fielding persuaded them to stay on as constables and even paid them a salary, or 'retainer', of 11s 6d (57p) a week. They were allowed up to 14s (70p) for expenses.

Fielding's office was in Bow Street Magistrates' Court and these constables became known as 'Bow Street Runners'. They wore no uniforms and soon their reputation was such that the majority of criminals feared them. They were essentially an early form of the Criminal Investigation Department (CID). When Henry Fielding died in 1754 his half-brother, Sir John Fielding, took over at Bow Street Court and soon established seven more magistrates' courts in the city, each with its own 'Runners' office. Sir John had been blind since birth and was known as 'The Blind Beak'; he was reputed to have known over three thousand criminals by the sound of their voices. Sir John formed the Bow Street Horse Patrol in 1763 – ten mounted men armed with truncheon, cutlass and pistol. These men patrolled an area of London within 6 miles of Charing Cross and became a familiar sight in their leather hats, blue coats with brass buttons, blue trousers and boots. They too were very successful at their job and eventually rid London of highwaymen. The government decided that they were no longer needed so the Horse Patrol was disbanded – with the result that the highwaymen returned!

About this time, in 1780, mass rioting broke out in London, known as the Gordon Riots. These riots, which lasted a whole week, were the culmination of public opposition to the granting of civil rights to Roman Catholics and were provoked by a petition to Parliament by Lord George Gordon against such rights.

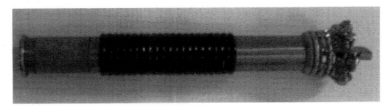

A tipstaff from the Georgian period carried as a badge of office by law enforcement officers of the day. The top unscrewed and the 'Bill of Warrant' was rolled up inside, giving the bearer the power of arrest. In order to effect an arrest the officer would touch the offender on the shoulder with the tipstaff – this is where the expression to be 'knocked off' or 'arrested' comes from. The modern term 'The Bill' used to describe the police also derives from this document. Tipstaves were eventually taken out of service in 1880; by this time the Bow Street Runners had long since been disbanded and the tipstaff was used only by plain-clothes CID officers and as a symbol of authority by very senior officers.

The Bow Street Runners carried a wooden truncheon not only as a weapon of defence but also as proof of identity. This painted truncheon dates back to just before the Victorian age. As a weapon of defence this style of truncheon was little match for the determined criminal, but for police officers it was the sole means of defending themselves for almost two hundred years more. The wooden truncheon of the Runner was held secure in a long, narrow pocket in one of the tails of his coat. The truncheon of a later force, the 'Peelers', was carried in a similar manner, in the coat tails, until truncheon pockets were sewn into the trouser leg.

Eventually the military was sent in to quell the trouble, but in the 'pacification' there were over two hundred people killed and two hundred and fifty wounded. The government was at last forced to provide a better-organised police force. Just before the reign of Victoria commenced a new Horse Patrol was formed, similar to its predecessor – with blue coats – but with red waistcoats; hence the officers acquired the nickname 'Robin Redbreasts'. With the increase in trade in and out of the port of London another new police force, called the 'Marine Police', was formed in 1798 to deal with crimes being committed on the River Thames and in the port of London.

A print of John Townsend, a famous Bow Street Runner. The Runners formed London's first band of organised regular police.

Sir Robert Peel, who as Home Secretary in 1829 formed the New Police force, later to be known as the Metropolitan Police. As Irish Secretary a few years previously Peel had restructured the Irish Police force, whose officers were to become known as 'Peelers' after their founder. Likewise, once the Metropolitan Police was formed, the officers of London were also known by this name. Peel is regarded as the founder of the British Police service.

SIR ROBERT PEEL

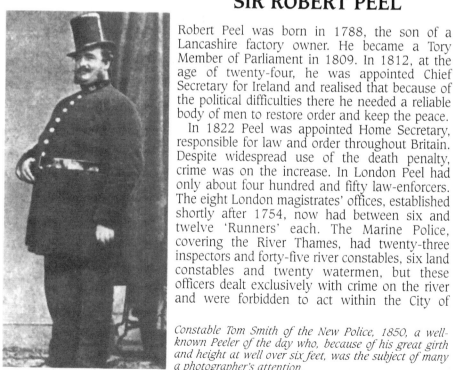

Robert Peel was born in 1788, the son of a Lancashire factory owner. He became a Tory Member of Parliament in 1809. In 1812, at the age of twenty-four, he was appointed Chief Secretary for Ireland and realised that because of the political difficulties there he needed a reliable body of men to restore order and keep the peace.

In 1822 Peel was appointed Home Secretary, responsible for law and order throughout Britain. Despite widespread use of the death penalty, crime was on the increase. In London Peel had only about four hundred and fifty law-enforcers. The eight London magistrates' offices, established shortly after 1754, now had between six and twelve 'Runners' each. The Marine Police, covering the River Thames, had twenty-three inspectors and forty-five river constables, six land constables and twenty watermen, but these officers dealt exclusively with crime on the river and were forbidden to act within the City of

Constable Tom Smith of the New Police, 1850, a well-known Peeler of the day who, because of his great girth and height at well over six feet, was the subject of many a photographer's attention.

Political correctness of the day being made fun of in a satirical cartoon ridiculing the idea of women being enlisted into the ranks of Peel's New Police! This notion had been discussed when Peel formed the Metropolitan Police but his forward-thinking plans were the subject of much derision. He had clearly been considering a very real need to provide female officers at some stage, but it was not until almost one hundred years later, in 1918, that uniformed female police officers were first to be seen on the streets of London.

Right: *This group of officers includes a sergeant (right) wearing the newly introduced helmet that replaced the top hat in the 1860s.*

Robert Peel's plan to introduce the New Police into London did not win the favour of every aspect of the community. He intended to wipe out all traces of the old policing systems, including the watchmen. This cartoon of the day pictures Peel taking on the 'Charlies'.

11

London. In addition to these officers there were the Bow Street Horse Patrol and Foot Patrols, along with the watchmen (still known as 'Charlies') and the inefficient parish constables.

Peel wanted to replace the old watch system with a more efficient and trained police service covering London under a single controlling body. A committee of enquiry was formed and supported Peel's plans. Peel put together a Bill to present to Parliament. 'My Bill', he said, 'enables the Secretary of State to abolish gradually the existing Watch establishments, to substitute in their room a Police force that shall act by day and by night. I propose to substitute the New Police gradually for the old one, not to attempt too much at first, to begin perhaps with ten or fifteen parishes in the city of Westminster and gradually to extend the Police District.' The one exception would be the City of London, which Peel wanted to retain the right to have its own police force.

In 1829 Peel eventually carried his Metropolitan Police Improvement Bill through both Houses of Parliament and it became law on 19th July. On 29th September the first thousand men of Peel's New Police went out on patrol in the capital. Peel made it known that he intended to abolish the Bow Street Runners, who were still operating at this time, though more as a detective agency than a police force. Peel also intended to absorb the Thames Police into the new Metropolitan Police. However, it was several years before the last of the Bow Street Runners and the 'Charlies' disappeared.

Peel appointed two new commissioners to take charge of his new police force. He chose two Irishmen: Colonel Charles Rowan and a barrister called Richard Mayne. They divided up the London area into divisions, sections and beats. The new force numbered just over one thousand men, including eight superintendents, twenty inspectors, eighty-eight sergeants and 895 constables.

The Commissioners think it right again to caution every man in the Police Force, at a time when an attempt is made to create a strong prejudice against them, that they should do their duty with every possible moderation and forbearance, and that they should not furnish a just ground of complaint against themselves by any misconduct. This caution is to be understood as applying to all occasions, but particularly to those on which they are called out in large bodies. It is highly desirable that the Constables should not use their truncheons in any manner that may cause annoyance or irritation, except when absolutely necessary.

Police Order – 1st November 1830

Then, as now, police officers were often reminded of the importance of conducting themselves in a professional and proper manner while on duty. However, one can only guess at how a police officer could effectively use his truncheon without causing 'irritation' to the unfortunate recipient!

Robert Peel (left), pictured with Richard Mayne. Mayne had been a barrister before being appointed one of the Commissioners of the Metropolitan Police to assist Colonel Charles Rowan in running the force. Mayne served from 1829 until 1868, having been the sole Commissioner since 1855.

Colonel Charles Rowan was one of the initial pair of Commissioners to take charge of the Metropolitan Police, along with Richard Mayne. He served as Commissioner from 1829 until 1850.

These constables wore a new uniform, were paid 1 guinea a week and had to be 'civil and obliging' to the public at all times. This must have been quite difficult on occasion because many Londoners resented being taxed for the privilege of their new police force, this tax being raised locally and not nationally. They felt that the old watch system was cheaper so therefore far more efficient, and many would not co-operate with the new police. Anti-police feeling resulted in a number of Peelers being assaulted and even

'Peel's Police', 'Raw Lobsters' and 'Blue Devils' were among the many names given to the New Police. Many people who preferred, for whatever reason, the old and ineffective system of watchmen and parish constables initially disliked this new police force. Public hatred and unrest, as this poster clearly indicates, were rife in certain sections of the community.

Peel's Police,
RAW LOBSTERS,
Blue Devils,

Or by whatever other appropriate Name they may be known.

Notice is hereby given,

That a Subscription has been entered into, to supply the **PEOPLE** with **STAVES** of a superior Effect, either for Defence or Punishment, which will be in readiness to be gratuitously distributed whenever a similar unprovoked, and therefore unmanly and blood-thirsty Attack, be again made upon Englishmen, by a Force unknown to the British Constitution, and called into existence by a Parliament illegally constituted, legislating for their individual interests, consequently in opposition to the Public good.

" Put not your trust in Princes."—DAVID
" Help yourself, and Heaven will help you."—FRENCH Motto.

murdered. The wealthy encouraged their coachmen to lash out at the Peelers or even run them down! There was talk in London of attacking the Prime Minister, Wellington, and assassinating both him and Peel, and it was widely alleged that 'Peel's Bloody Gang' had been issued with six thousand cutlasses from the Tower of London.

Police officers were made to pay for failed prosecutions if any of their offenders were found 'not guilty'. If a policeman could not pay the fees, he would be sent to the debtors' prison. Jurors were sometimes hostile to the police and on one occasion, when trying a man for murdering a police officer, they returned a verdict of 'justifiable homicide'. It was little surprise that many Peelers resigned; out of the three thousand officers who had joined the force since its inception in 1829 only six hundred were still in post

Above: *Cutlasses such as this one, based on the naval pattern, were issued to police officers, but despite training in their use officers were under threat of disciplinary action if they ever used them. A Metropolitan Police Order of 1832 decreed that 'The Police Constable is to be given to understand distinctly that the sword is put into his hand merely as a defensive weapon in case his life should be in danger, and that he shall not use or even draw it for any less weighty cause; he will be called to strict account and will most probably be dismissed'.*

The first police whistles were introduced in London in 1884 following extensive trials against the former rattle. The whistle was found to be a far more effective means of communication in a city in which the nearest policeman should be within earshot of the whistle call for assistance.

With only a wooden truncheon to defend himself, the patrolling policeman was a vulnerable target for the more ruthless criminal of the day. The question of arming the police with firearms was raised in the early years of the New Police but there was then, as now, great opposition to the routine arming of officers.

when Victoria came to the throne eight years later.

Eventually the public became used to the Peelers. They accepted that they were there to uphold the law and soon realised that they were armed only with wooden truncheons. Indeed, when a Peeler was stabbed to death in Holborn the public held a collection for his widow and family.

With the favour and respect of the public won, the image of the Peeler improved and he was seen as a humane and decent public servant, as this popular contemporary image shows.

15

Every morning, night-duty officers who had made arrests during the previous night were obliged to stay on duty in order to parade their various prisoners before the magistrates' court. Only when the court case was over could the officer go to bed for the day before recommencing his duty that evening. Officers marching their prisoners to court in the mornings were a common sight.

THE 'PEELERS' – THE NEW POLICE

At the beginning of the Victorian era the 'Peelers' were still serving as the New Police only in London. The rural counties and boroughs throughout the rest of the country continued to rely upon their locally appointed old-fashioned parish constables for law enforcement.

Peel's men went about their duties in an efficient and competent manner, dealing with a variety of matters, including dog stealing, runaway apprentices, bigamy, furious driving, stealing dead bodies and pickpockets, to name but a few. Half of the new police force was on duty from 9 p.m. until 6 a.m. and the other half took over during the daytime. Later the proportion of men working at night was reduced to a third. These men patrolled their beat at a pace of 2½ miles per hour and were strictly forbidden to lean on anything or to sit down. In the opinion of the Duke of Wellington, these 'New Police' looked very 'respectable'.

One of the new police officers was a Constable Cavanagh. In his memoirs he described the moment he first put on his new blue uniform:

When I looked at myself in the glass with the uniform on for the first time, I wondered what could have led me to take the final step of becoming a 'Peeler'. I had to put on a swallow tail coat, and a rabbit-skin high top hat, covered with

'Duty and Pleasure', drawn in 1872. This illustration shows the uniform after 1865. The truncheon is visible, which was not unusual. By the time of the drawing, the streets were lit by gas.

16

Manchester Peelers relaxing with churchwarden pipes in about 1850.

BOROUGH OF TIVERTON.

POLICEMAN
WANTED.

An Active Young Man between 25 and 35 Years of Age, Height not under 5 feet 9 inches, is required in the Police Force of this Borough. *Salary 19s. per Week.*

TESTIMONIALS TO CHARACTER must be sent to the Town Clerk's Office, on or before Tuesday the 10th of August next, and Applicants are desired to attend at the Guildhall, on Wednesday the 11th of August at Eleven o'clock in the Forenoon.

By order of the Watch Committee.

C. M. HOLE,
TOWN CLERK.

HEAD, PRINTER, GOLD STREET, TIVERTON.

Left: *In 1946 the Tiverton Borough Police in Devon was one of the last rural borough forces in Britain to be amalgamated into its own county constabulary. This 'Policeman Wanted' poster is somewhat scant in information compared to modern recruitment packs!*

Below: *This print shows a superintendent and two inspectors of the former Devon County Constabulary in 1871. Officers of the county forces often wore no insignia other than their ornate frock-coats to signify rank and status.*

leather, weighing eighteen ounces; a pair of Wellington boots, the leather of which must have been at least a sixteenth of an inch thick, and a belt about four inches broad, with a great buckle some six inches deep.... My hat was slipping all over my head; my boots, which were two sizes too large, were rubbing the skin off my heels; and the stock was a thick leather one, and four inches deep; was nearly choking me. I would have given all I possessed to have got back into my ordinary clothes

The officers who formed the first Peelers in 1829 reported to the Foundling Hospital on 26th September that year, a few days before going out on patrol, to be issued with their uniform and equipment.

A sergeant and three constables of the Devon Constabulary in 1871. The constables in this remote and rural force wore knapsacks in which they carried their equipment on the long marches around their beats. A rural constable often marched over 30 miles a day around his area, in all weathers.

Below: *Pictured in 1864 at Epsom Races are Superintendent Robert Walker (mounted) and (left to right) Inspector David Baldry, who served at Buckingham Palace, Inspector Eleazar Denning, who was in charge of the parliamentary police at the House of Commons, and Constable Donald Swanson, who later rose through the ranks to become a superintendent and played a leading part in the investigations into the notorious 'Jack the Ripper' murders. They are wearing the new style of tunic, which had dispensed with the long tails.*

Clothing went through great changes during the times of the Peelers and it would be difficult to detail the exact appearance of these new officers. The commissioners wore no uniforms; the superintendents and inspectors bought uniforms at their own expense.

On the collar of the policeman's uniform appeared a number. This number was his divisional identity number and was, quite understandably, referred to as a 'collar number'. It is rather an anomaly that this number is still referred to by the same name although it now appears on an officer's shoulder epaulette instead of on his collar. In many of the larger police forces, such as the Metropolitan Police, an officer was also given a unique service number, similar to those of the military. The divisional number on the collar sometimes had the alphabetical letter of the geographical division in which the officer served. This number would change if he were to be removed to another divisional area, but his unique service number remained the same throughout his career.

The sergeants might have worn chevrons on their arms, but this is not mentioned in early records. Like the constables, the sergeants wore a blue tailed coat with metal buttons and a heavy top hat with a deep nap surface. Winter trousers were made of the same cloth as the coat, but in summer the fabric was thinner and the trousers were of a lighter colour, probably grey. The heavy greatcoat was made of brown cloth and a cape was worn in wet weather.

Right: *A constable of the Norwich City Police c.1850. The band on his left arm is a duty band, worn to signify that the officer was on duty. In many police forces at that time constables were required to wear their uniforms even when off duty, so there was little means of telling whether or not an officer was on duty. It is rare to find the duty band worn around the upper arm like this as opposed to around the left cuff.*

Above: *Restraining a violent prisoner has always presented a challenge to the police service. The original type of restraint was basically a large wooden toggle with a loop of cord, which was put over the offender's wrists and twisted. More and more elaborate means of restraint were developed throughout the nineteenth century, until eventually this style of handcuffs, made by the Hyatt Company of Birmingham, was brought into use. Such handcuffs remained in service for over a hundred years until further developments came about with the introduction of chromed ratchet handcuffs, which could be snapped on to an offender's wrist in seconds. However, Hyatt remains one of the world's leading manufacturers of restraints.*

The following list details the various components, with prices, of the uniform issued in those early days of the Peelers.

Blue coat	£1 5s 6d
Collar	2s 6d
Dress trousers	14s 6d
Undress trousers	9s 3d
Greatcoat	£1 15s 5d
Collar badge for greatcoat	8d
Cape	5s 6d
Hat	12s
Boots	12s 6d

There is no mention of gloves in these early records, but in 1840 the police were referred to in a letter as 'these fine fellows in white gloves'. At this time the cost of fully equipping a policeman was £6.

The equipment issued to the police in 1829 consisted of batons, rattles (whistles were not used until 1884), lanterns, handcuffs and small numbers of cutlasses, sword-belts and pistols. Initially lanterns were issued to all officers but in order to cut costs this practice was withdrawn and they were leased from a contractor who was paid 6d per week to supply and fuel lanterns. By 1833 there were 1062 lanterns in use in the winter and five hundred in the summer. Bullseye lanterns

Officers from the Bristol City Police practising their cutlass drill in the mid 1870s. The cutlass was not issued in Bristol as a standard piece of equipment but, as in many other forces, a supply of them was kept at major police stations in case of public disturbances.

An officer of the Scarborough Borough Police pictured c.1860. Clearly shown is the standard-issue bullseye lantern hanging from the officer's belt. He is wearing the new-style comb helmet, which replaced the top hat; it took its name from the cock's comb as it had a ridge all the way down the back, as on a fireman's helmet. Many police forces, including the City of London Police, still favour the comb helmet.

Below: *A poster from 1840 requesting information about a murder in Leicestershire. Appeals to the public for information about serious crimes are not new, although a royal pardon for accomplices is not so common these days.*

£.200. REWARD.

MURDEROUS OUTRAGES.

Whereas it appears that Three several cases of SHOOTING with Murderous Intent at Individuals Travelling on the Turnpike Roads in this County have recently occurred, namely:

Mr. JOHN PRATT, on the Loughborough Road, on the night of the 27th October, the Ball passing through his Hat.

Mr. THOMAS OLDACRES, on the Hinckley road, on the night of the 18th November, the Shot not taking effect.

Mr. WILLIAM BURDETT, also, on the Hinckley road, on the night of the 18th November, the Ball lodging in his Shoulder.

Now Notice is hereby given, that
A REWARD OF

ONE HUNDRED POUNDS

Will be paid to any person or persons who shall give such information as shall lead to the Conviction of the party or parties guilty of any one of these Outrages:

AND THAT

THE MARQUESS OF NORMANBY

One of her Majesty's principal Secretaries of State, Has authorized the Magistrates to declare, that a Reward of

ONE HUNDRED POUNDS

Will be paid by the Government

(In addition to that above offered) to any Person who shall give such information and evidence as shall lead to the discovery and conviction of the Person or Persons concerned in either of the three attempts above described.

And LORD NORMANBY further states,

That he will advise the grant of Her Majesty's gracious Pardon to any Accomplice (not being the person who actually fired the gun or pistol in either case) who shall give such evidence as shall lead to the same result.

FREDERICK GOODYER,
CHIEF CONSTABLE

County Police Office, Leicester, 28th November, 1840.

Above: *Rattles were issued to police officers from 1829 until 1884 and were used to summon assistance or to raise an alarm. One thousand rattles manufactured by Parkers of Holborn were ordered for the New Police in 1829. In 1883 they were tested against whistles and proved less effective. It was found that the whistle was clearly audible for 900 yards (820 metres) and so the rattle, with a far shorter range, was taken out of service. However, rattles did make a brief comeback during the Second World War when they were used to sound the alarm in case of a German gas attack.*

The strictures placed upon police officers were too much for many to bear and the police service lost many officers through seemingly ridiculous rules and regulations, as illustrated in this Lancaster poster.

COUNTY OF LANCASTER CONSTABULARY FORCE.

THE FOLLOWING MAXIMS

Are to be strictly observed and born in mind by the Constables of the Force.

1. Constables are placed in authority to PROTECT, not to OPPRESS, the PUBLIC.
2. To do which effectually, they must earnestly and systematically exert themselves to PREVENT CRIME.
3. When a Crime has been committed, no time should be lost, nor exertions spared, to discover and bring to justice the OFFENDERS.
4. Obtain a knowledge of all REPUTED THIEVES, and IDLE and DISORDERLY PERSONS.
5. Watch narrowly all Persons having NO VISIBLE MEANS OF SUBSISTENCE.
6. Prevent VAGRANCY.
7. Be IMPARTIAL in the discharge of duties.
8. Discard from the mind all POLITICAL and SECTARIAN prejudices.
9. Be COOL and INTREPID in the discharge of duties in emergencies and unavoidable conflicts.
10. Avoid ALTERCATIONS, and display PERFECT COMMAND of TEMPER under INSULT and gross PROVOCATION, to which all Constables must occasionally be liable.
11. NEVER STRIKE, but in SELF-DEFENCE, nor treat a Prisoner with more Rigour than may be absolutely necessary to prevent escape.
12. Practice the most complete SOBRIETY, one instance of DRUNKENNESS will render a Constable liable to DISMISSAL.
13. Treat with the utmost CIVILITY all classes of HER MAJESTY'S SUBJECTS, and cheerfully render ASSISTANCE to all in need of it.
14. Exhibit DEFERENCE and RESPECT to the MAGISTRACY.
15. Promptly and cheerfully OBEY all SUPERIOR OFFICERS.
16. Render an HONEST, FAITHFUL, and SPEEDY account of all MONIES and PROPERTY, whether intrusted with them for others, or taken possession of in the execution of duty.
17. With reference to the foregoing, bear especially in mind that "HONESTY IS THE BEST POLICY."
18. Be perfectly neat and clean in Person and Attire.
19. Never sit down in a PUBLIC HOUSE or BEER SHOP.
20. AVOID TIPPLING.
21. It is the interest of every man to devote some portion of his spare time to the practice of READING and WRITING and the general improvement of his mind.
22. IGNORANCE is an insuperable bar to promotion.

J. WOODFORD

came into use towards the end of the 1830s. In 1840 a bullseye lantern cost 7 shillings. Rattles were carried in the breast pocket over the heart in order to protect against knife attacks. In several recorded incidents the life of a Peeler was saved when the rattle deflected a blade.

In November 1830 twelve policemen at Scotland Yard were armed with cutlasses for office guarding and in 1832 the Home Office gave permission for policemen based at remote country stations to be so armed if reinforcements could not be provided quickly. Cutlasses were not generally issued to policemen on routine patrol in cities. In 1834 each inspector had a pocket pistol, and from 1884 to as late as 1936 constables on patrol in 'outer divisions' could, with their superintendent's permission, carry a firearm. An uncertain number of handcuffs were issued to police officers as part of their routine equipment.

Constable Cavanagh gave unemployment as a reason for wanting to join the police force: 'I had been out of employment for a long time and made up my mind to get into the police... or take the Queen's shilling [join the Army]. I was fortunate enough, with thirty-six others out of 140 applicants, to get on.' Some might have joined because the discipline or outdoor life appealed; maybe others had been policemen's sons. Perhaps the biggest advantage of joining the police force was the security it offered.

There were many disadvantages suffered by the Victorian policeman. Physically the work was very demanding. A constable on night duty walked on average 20 miles a night, in all weather conditions, seven days a week. Constant patrolling in unsuitable boots often injured the police officer's feet and legs. On one occasion in Derbyshire a constable was caught by his sergeant with a boot off. His excuse that he had a sore foot was not accepted and he was dismissed! Until the end of Victoria's reign, a police officer was not entitled to any refreshment breaks or hot meals. If he was wet at the start of his shift, he stayed

The Derbyshire County Constabulary Chief Constable of 1875 obviously felt that an error had been made in recruiting poor Constable Harper!

wet until his duty ended. London was a most unhealthy place to work. With its open sewers, more police officers died from tuberculosis than from being attacked by thugs. London was also an industrial city with factories and houses burning poor-quality coal, which caused terrible winter smogs.

The police authorities knew full well what was happening and in 1856 the City of London Police Surgeon reported that men were being worn out by the job. He wrote: 'By the term "Worn Out" made use of in my certificates I would wish to imply that such officers... are prematurely aged and suffer from defective physical strength and other bodily infirmities.' This was in spite of the fact that when recruits joined the police force they were of above-average physical ability and in good health.

The police officer's pay was another matter of complaint. A superintendent received £200 per year, an inspector £100, a sergeant about £58 and a constable £54 12s per year, or 3s (15p) per day. (The difference between a sergeant's pay and a senior constable's pay was very little.) Indeed, at the start of Victoria's reign a constable could receive as little as 17s 6d (87p) per week after deductions for rent and pension. A police constable's pay was roughly equivalent to that of a sailor, quarryman or gamekeeper. They earned more than farm labourers but less than many other working men, such as postmen and miners. They did have the right to be considered for a pension but this was at the discretion of the commissioner. Sometimes a man with twenty years' service or more could have his pension refused because of some minor indiscretion committed many years previously. Unfortunately many men did not survive long enough to draw their pensions. After 1862 the Metropolitan Police paid pensions to men who had served for fifteen years, with an increased sum for anyone who had served longer.

Discipline was intolerably strict. Policemen were dismissed if a member of the public complained about them or if they committed any offence, kept bad company or broke police regulations such as being late on duty, being improperly dressed or absconding from a beat. The usual cause for dismissal was being drunk. An early commissioner dismissed in one go an inspector with twenty-eight years' service and sixty other men for drinking at Christmas against his

A Metropolitan Police group in the mid 1860s. A new eight-buttoned coat replaced the old-style swallowtail coat and a cock's comb helmet replaced the top hat. The cock's comb helmet seen in this photograph was replaced in 1870 with the six-panelled helmet, a similar version of which was still in use in 2003. As can be seen, the fashion of the day was to wear beards.

orders. In 1879 the same commissioner declared that 'the offence of drunkenness is less severely dealt with than it used to be'.

Even so, the Victorian policeman was under much stricter control and regulations than other working men, and this caused a lot of disquiet in the force. There were attempts to start a trade union in 1862, but men involved in this uprising were imprisoned and dismissed from the force. In 1890 some men went on strike and they too were dismissed for their plans to form a union. It was not until 1919, shortly after the national police strike of 1918 and long after the Victorian age, that the police union, the Police Federation, was created. Police officers were kept well out of politics. It was not until 1887 that an officer was allowed to vote.

The Metropolitan Police was also responsible for providing Royal Protection Officers, wherever in Britain the member of the royal family needing protection might be. The officer would be assigned on a personal basis and would travel wherever his ward should go. In a similar manner, the force was also responsible for protecting senior politicians and ambassadors – this system still remains today.

Sir Robert Peel's New Police, formed in 1829, had become accepted and it was therefore time, Parliament thought, to see to it that the rest of Britain was provided with a similarly constituted police force. The Municipal Corporations Act of 1835 set about instigating this. The Peelers had policed London for six years and now, at last, the rest of the country was about to follow suit.

Sergeant-Major Piddick of the Devon County Constabulary teaching quarter-staff drill to the daughters of Mr Gerald de Courcey-Hamilton, Chief Constable of Devon c.1860. Sergeant-Major Piddick was in charge of training police recruits at their headquarters and as such would more than likely have been in regular contact with the Chief Constable. Perhaps Mr de Courcey-Hamilton felt that his daughters required some training and discipline!

POLICING THE COUNTIES AND BOROUGHS

The new Metropolitan Police force, as it was now known, which had been formed by Peel, covered only London; the remainder of the country continued with its old policing systems of justices and parish constables. It was clear that in rural areas the old style of policing was still operating reasonably well, but in the industrial towns and cities, where crime and lawlessness spread rapidly among the slums, there was a great need for reform. In 1834 the city of Liverpool had a population of 250,000, with only fifty night watchmen to maintain law and order!

The Municipal Corporations Act of 1835 was passed, compelling boroughs and

The rank of sergeant-major in the police service was rare indeed. This Cornish photograph of the 1880s shows the rank insignia of four inverted chevrons and a crown on the right cuff. The sergeant-major was responsible for training recruits, as this train-ing-school photograph taken at Bodmin Police Headquarters shows.

cities outside London to form their own police forces. Once Victoria had come to the throne in 1837 this requirement was extended to the counties. However, many counties did not readily adopt the new instructions and it took some years before the last of the old 'parish constable' systems died out.

The new town and borough authorities constituted to form police forces were called 'corporations'. They were allowed to set up their new police force as they saw fit. Some modelled their police on the Metropolitan force but not all took such action and many authorities refused to undertake such an expensive exercise. Indeed, three years after the 1835 Act, only half the boroughs in England and Wales had a police force and it was not until 1862 that the last of the counties (Rutland) had formed its own force.

The Victorian version of the modern-day Police Authority, responsible for overseeing and controlling a police force, was called the 'Watch Committee'. Watch Committee members were appointed by the town or borough corporation, and they in turn appointed the chief constable (the senior rank in a county police force). The Metropolitan Police was directly answerable to the Home Office, and the 'chief constable' of the Metropolitan Police was called the commissioner. The City of London Police also had a commissioner, who was answerable to and appointed by the Corporation of the City of London. Everywhere else in England and Wales had a system of policing with an identical rank structure and responsibilities. The chief constable was the senior officer in charge of the force. He would have a deputy to assist him. In the nineteenth century many rural police forces appointed a superintendent to take on this deputy's role. The formal ranks of deputy and assistant chief constable are relatively new and did not exist in Victorian times.

Each police force was divided up into geographical areas known as 'divisions'. In charge of each division was a super-intendent, and under him in rank were the inspectors. An inspector would be in charge of a large police station, which might have a few smaller village and town stations in its control. Under the in-spectors were the sergeants, who would

This photograph of c. 1880 shows a sergeant with constables of the Devon Constabulary.

Constable George White of King's Lynn had previously served as a local parish constable like many officers of his generation who had simply transferred to their county force. This photograph taken in the 1850s shows him in uniform, clearly not far from the end of his service.

be in charge of a 'section'. That section might consist of a group of constables, perhaps ten or more in a large town station, or five or six village constables in remote rural areas.

When a constable first joined a police force he would be referred to as a 'third class constable'. He would attend training and guidance of a basic nature but would soon be out on his own patrolling within the public. Police forces differed slightly, but generally a constable would be given a chevron stripe to wear on his cuff after two years. This would usually be worn upside-down, with the point facing upwards. He would have a small increase in salary to reflect his two-year service. After a further two years he would be given a second stripe and be referred to as a 'second class constable', with an additional increase in wages. This simply reflected the constable's length of service again, rather than indicating any seniority of rank. After another five years, if his conduct were appropriate, he would be upgraded to a 'first class constable', the highest constable grade with the highest pay. He would now wear three upside-down chevrons on his cuff. A constable could not seek promotion to the rank of sergeant unless he had been a 'first class constable'. The ranks of chief superintendent and chief inspector were not introduced until the twentieth century.

Promotions were dealt with by way of a constable taking a written examination, usually consisting of reading and writing as well as mathematics

Constable John Cousins, pictured in the 1870s with his wife and eight daughters in the rear yard of their police cottage at Halwill in Devon. He is wearing the Prussian pickelhaube-style helmet that the Devon Constabulary wore at the end of the nineteenth century. Constable Cousins went on to serve at Barnstaple in north Devon, where his two sons were born.

The Kent County Constabulary Cycle Section was formed in 1896. Its cycles were purchased for 8 guineas each. These officers were not stationed at any particular police house in a rural area but were rather a 'county resource' to be used 'where more mobile constables could be utilised'.

and law. It would be very rare for an officer with less than fifteen years of service ever to be promoted to the rank of sergeant. Usually a senior military officer, and not a police officer who had come up through the ranks, would fill the post of chief constable. This system of appointing chief constables lasted well into the twentieth century.

There were no medals given exclusively to police officers; these were generally introduced after the reign of Victoria – notably the King's Police Medal (now the Queen's Police Medal) for distinguished service. Police Constable William Cole won the Albert Medal for bravery in 1885 when he carried a Sinn Fein bomb from the Palace of Westminster. He was injured when it exploded.

Likewise, the reward and recognition for gallantry was only given locally, with the commendation or merit system. A chief constable could give an officer a certificate of commendation for an act of excellent duty or bravery. Usually that commendation comprised a certificate and nothing else. However, one incident in the city of Exeter impressed the Watch Committee so much that the Exeter City Police force introduced the 'commendation star'. In the 1860s a serious fire at a theatre in Exeter risked claiming many lives. The fire brigades at this time were combined police/fire services, manned by constables. The fire service rescued many people and the Watch Committee requested that a medal be struck to reward the heroism of those involved. This request was refused, so instead they had a large gold star embroidered and sewn on to the sleeves of the officers' tunics as a mark of recognition. Despite numerous force amalgamations this system has remained in the Devon and Cornwall Constabulary as the rarest, but highest, commendation that the chief constable can award, usually for bravery. Numerous other police forces followed suit and now have similar badges and crests sewn on to the sleeves of their tunics.

The conditions endured by the rural policeman were as bad as those of his colleagues in the Metropolitan force. In one rural county police force the chief constable set out three pages of strictures relating to the required dress of officers and men in his force. A police officer was issued with one uniform each year and was given the opportunity to purchase his uniform from the previous year to use as second best. Many of the constables would, no doubt, have found it difficult to raise the half crown required for a greatcoat or 1s 4d for a tunic.

Policemen often resorted to other means to help out with family bills, and the

Many police forces had, and indeed a few still do have, their own bands. The Metropolitan Police had divisional bands as well as a combined band, which was significantly larger. Bands and police choirs have unfortunately diminished with time and progress. This picture shows the S Division Band in the 1880s.

Until the Second World War most police forces were combined police fire brigades and the chief constables also took on the role of Chief Fire Officer. This picture from the 1880s shows the Oswestry Police Fire Brigade.

force acknowledged their desire to keep livestock and fowls. A police order of November 1876 stated that 'A list of all members of the Force residing in station houses having permission to keep fowls etc.... is to be sent to Headquarters with names, stations and by whom authorised'. Monthly 'Pay Parades' were held at Divisional Headquarters. Men from the villages had to march to their superintendent at the Divisional Headquarters to receive their wages. The traditions of the Pay Parade remained for eighty years in some constabularies. Attending church on Sunday was regarded as a duty, and questions would be

In 1858 the Metropolitan Police obtained its first horse-drawn prison cart to transport prisoners to the local cells. By 1885 the force had eight such vehicles. These were called 'Black Marias', their name taken from a large and powerful black lodging-house keeper called Maria Lee, who lived in Massachusetts in the United States in the 1830s. She often used to help police officers manhandle disorderly drunks to the police station; hence the expression 'we're sending for Black Maria'.

The rear of the Black Maria was divided up into small cells, each of which could hold one prisoner in a seated position. The door to the cell had a small flap for the gaoler to open if necessary. Bow Street Magistrates' Court had a special reception area from which the Black Maria would unload prisoners into the court cells.

The inspectors for the Home District, appointed under the Prisons Act of 1835, could barely conceal their horror at what went on inside the Black Marias, reporting thus: 'They are 8 feet 4 inches long, 4 feet 5 inches wide and 5 feet 5 inches high, and will each conveniently accommodate about twenty prisoners, but upwards of thirty are occasionally conveyed. No officer, either male or female, is inside the van. It can excite no surprises that, under such circumstances, scenes of gross indecency constantly occur. We have ourselves been frequently present when the van has reached the prison where wretched characters, of both sexes, after being thus mingled together, descend from that carriage with clothing not sufficient to cover their nakedness.'

raised if an officer were ever caught out of uniform, even in church.

In an instruction from his Bodmin headquarters in 1868, the Chief Constable of Cornwall insisted that 'In making out the new conference sheets care is to be taken to make every night conference at the houses of the nobility, gentry, clergy and principal ratepayers or at such buildings and places as would be likely to offer temptation to burglars'. Before the days of radios the sergeant and superintendent needed to know where, at any time, a constable would be on his beat. Therefore 'conference points' were set up, at which the constable was required to show at set times, and it was a serious disciplinary offence to fail to make any of these points without good reason.

Generally the only rank that rode a horse at this time was the superintendent in the county forces. Usually a senior constable, perhaps nearing retirement, was appointed as groom and he looked after the 'county horse' for the superintendent. The horse was usually not owned by the police force but was more likely to be

A mounted officer dashes to the assistance of a young lady. Dealing with runaway horses was quite a time-consuming occupation for patrolling police officers and numerous instances of gallantry awards are recorded for such daring rescues as this one in Hyde Park.

The Manchester Police Ambulance Service, 1900. This service was run by the Manchester Police from 1895 until 1948.

shared with the local corporation. Indeed in the borough of Tiverton in Devon the superintendent had access to his horse only when the corporation did not need it for hauling the corporation rubbish cart! Some city police forces, however, did have a mounted horse section, and these horses were owned by the force.

Sergeants and inspectors were given an allowance to have a pedal cycle for duty purposes, but it was rare indeed to find a cycle being used for duty by a constable. There were perks to being on duty with a cycle, as a member of the police cyclist section in the 1880s would testify. The cyclist section in some forces was used to catch young men who were speeding and riding furiously on their cycles. For this 'exhausting' duty an officer was paid an extra shilling a week for danger money!

It sometimes seemed as if the Victorian police constable had to devote all aspects of his life to the force. In the event of a female being taken into custody the constable's wife would be needed to act as gaoler and matron for little or no financial recompense. Even the cleaning of the police stations was the responsibility of the constable.

The New Police head-quarters at 4 Whitehall Place, London. The back of the building opened on to a courtyard that had been the site of a residence owned by the kings of Scotland and known as 'Scotland Yard'.

BUILDINGS

The task of organising and designing the New Police was undertaken at the headquarters of the new force at 4 Whitehall Place, London. The headquarters remained at this site until 1890, when they were removed to premises on the Victoria Embankment. In 1967 the buildings were deemed too small to be of use and 'Scotland Yard' moved again.

One of London's most famous police stations is at Bow Street. Construction of the new purpose-built Bow Street police court and station, with accommodation for the 106 unmarried constables, was started in 1878 and completed in 1881. This station was the site of the first police office, later known as an 'enquiry office'.

In 1861 blue lamps were introduced outside police stations, but Queen Victoria objected to having this distressing reminder of the blue room in which Prince

The headquarters of the Metropolitan Police were moved in 1890 to premises on the Victoria Embankment known as 'New Scotland Yard'. In 1967 further relocation took place to a larger and more modern building at Broadway, SW1, also known as 'New Scotland Yard'.

31

Left: *Bow Street Police Court, drawn c.1845.*

Above: *The Marine Police on the Thames had been formed many years before the Metropolitan force but were soon subsumed into it after 1829. The 'Thames Division' of the Metropolitan Police was created with river police stations at Wapping and also on the Embankment, as this scene of 1899 shows. To this day the river Thames is still policed by the 'Thames Division', which has retained the small pontoon station on the Embankment as an operational base.*

Albert died confronting her whenever she visited the Opera House. Bow Street therefore became the only London police station to have a white rather than a blue lamp.

The oldest police station in Britain that is still operational is situated at Lutterworth in Leicestershire. In 1843 the police station and courthouse were erected on Gilmorton Road in

Police-station enquiry offices were few and far between in the Victorian era apart from in the larger cities. Even those urban facilities were very basic and were little more than a 'shop-front' (above), or occasionally an office (right), with an officer available to answer questions. They were not open twenty-four hours a day as are modern city offices. The photograph on the right shows the layout of a typical Victorian charge office as displayed at the Greater Manchester Police Museum.

The Bow Street magistrates had developed an anomalous legal independence, with no statutory basis for their authority. This set-up was ended by the 1839 Metropolitan Police Act, which defined them as stipendiary magistrates like the others. Nevertheless, Bow Street continued to be seen as the premier London magistrates' court, and committal proceedings for great criminal cases such as that of Dr Crippen continued to take place at Bow Street.

Right: *There has been a police station in Lutterworth, Leicestershire, since 1843 and it is claimed to be the oldest operational station in Britain.*

this town. Construction of the Tavistock police station and court in Devon closely followed eighteen months later. Erected from the ruins of the old abbey, with parts dating back to AD 910, Tavistock is also still an operational station.

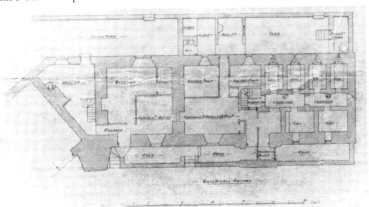

These plans of Tavistock station in Devon show a typical layout of a Victorian police station, with cells and offices. The building was converted from old stables and storage buildings in order to replace the old Guildhall, which was a one-roomed building unsuitable for the new parish police force. The room occupied by the constables is shown as 'Weights & Measures'; the police at this time were responsible for duties now undertaken by the Trading Standards Department, including checking weights and measures at shops and licensed premises.

In the days of the Bow Street Runners and Horse Patrol the lock-ups around the London area could barely contain the number of highwaymen taken into custody. As police building programmes progressed the village lock-up became redundant and most were demolished during the early years of Victoria's reign. Rare examples such as this one in Cranford, Middlesex – saved in the 1950s from the threat of demolition by a far-sighted local architect and councillor, John Blake – have been preserved and can be visited. The Cranford lock-up was built in 1810, reputedly on the site of a former Georgian lock-up. Records exist of it being used until 1860, when a number of people were incarcerated in it for taking part in a cockfight, an activity that had been outlawed in 1848.

Isolated rural villages at this time still retained their old 'lock-ups', many of which were available to house arrested criminals. The lock-up was a lasting bastion of the old parish constable days, first established even before these times. Most had originated during the last few years of the eighteenth century as a means of locking up criminals, particularly highwaymen, before they were taken to court. Some were barely more than a stone shed with a bench and no sanitation; others were slightly more elaborate. The lock-ups were maintained by the Vestry Committee of the local parish, this committee also being responsible for appointing the local parish constables in the days before the borough and county

In rural counties, after the establishment of the counties' own police forces, constables lived in rented cottages in villages. These officers were issued with large signs to hang over their front doors to signify that the building was the constable's house. This photograph shows the Devon Constabulary sign over the front door of Tavistock police station. When a lease on a cottage expired the constable would simply move to other premises, taking his sign with him. Various police forces had a variety of sign types. Many included a small slot into which a metal plate bearing the officer's collar number could be inserted, thus identifying which constable lived there.

Above left: *The cell corridor of Tavistock police station, showing the now disused cells. A prisoner was drowned after the cells were flooded in 1890 when the river Tavy, to the rear of the station, burst its banks. The new cells at the station were built in 1892 and are still in use. At the end of the cell passageway there is a small door leading to a narrow and steep flight of steps that goes right up into the dock of the magistrates' court above the cells.*

Above right: *The cell at the Tetbury Police Museum in Gloucestershire. Like many other Victorian constructions, the cells are extremely secure. The doors have steel-lined frames and two-and-a-half-turn locks. One visitor to the museum recounted that he had lived in the building for some time between the wars, when his father was the sergeant in charge. He told how his mother always kept bread and cheese for passing vagrants, and how the birch had stood outside the cells in a bucket of water to keep the twigs supple in order to administer the 'short sharp shock' according to the verdict of the magistrates upstairs.*

police forces. The local constable, who would have lived nearby in the parish in rented accommodation, was responsible for feeding the prisoner being held. He must have regarded this duty as a minor inconvenience compared with the alternative of having to take his prisoner many miles to a larger police office that had its own cells. These small lock-ups were a useful addition in the early days of law enforcement and although a throw-back to the medieval days they continued in use at isolated parishes well into the reign of Victoria.

As demands on policing grew the buildings changed to accommodate an expanding service. Many larger stations included a stable block for the superintendent's horse, if the constabulary owned the animal. Many had small bedrooms in their attics to accommodate the unmarried constables who served there. All stations were equipped with cells of some type. The smaller stations might have had just one small cell, big enough for an offender to sit in, but the larger city stations usually had bigger cell blocks, or 'Bridewells' as they were then called. Bridewell was a district of London between Fleet Street and the Thames, so-called after the nearby well of St Bride or St Bridget. Bridewells are named after a house of correction (built in 1829 and demolished in 1864) that stood in the vicinity of the Holy Well of St Bride. Similar houses of correction, as well as cells, were set up in other cities and these too became known as Bridewells.

Metropolitan officers in plain clothes pictured in about 1880. Apparently they were disguised in order not to stand out in a crowd!

THE DETECTIVES

There were no detectives in the Metropolitan Police for the first thirteen years, but this did not mean that there were no plain-clothes policemen. Officers in plain, or what was called 'coloured', clothing were used very early on. However, the public and many magistrates did not approve of this practice; in fact one magistrate dismissed all cases that involved a police constable who had been in plain clothes! Lord Melbourne, who succeeded Sir Robert Peel as Home Secretary, saw officers in plain clothes as a good idea and even made an order demanding their use, especially at political meetings where revolutionary activities might be revealed.

In 1842 an experiment was undertaken to introduce plain-clothes policemen who had no other uniform responsibilities or duties. Two inspectors and six sergeants were appointed for this purpose, their salaries being £200 and £73 respectively. The names of those original detectives were Inspectors Nicholas Pearce (a former Bow Street Runner) and John Hayes, and Sergeants William Gerret, Stephen Thornton, Jonathan Whicher, Charles Goff, Frederick Shaw and Frederick Braddick. Whilst engaged on enquiries they would 'adopt civilian clothing associated with an occupation'. The Commissioner, Rowan, explained the plan to the then Home Secretary, Sir James Graham, in the following letter:

> The Commissioners intend that each individual of the branch of police proposed to be formed when not immediately occupied in pursuit of offenders should be employed in gaining information as to the facilities that might be afforded from time to time for the commission of

This photograph shows the police team of uniformed officers and detectives who investigated the 'Moat Farm Murder' in Clavering, Essex, when Samuel Dougal murdered his mistress in 1899 and buried her body in the garden. The officers in the photograph are (back, left to right) Constables Field and Lindsey with (front, left to right) Sergeant Scott and Constable Fell. The little dog was called Jacko and belonged to the murdered woman, Camille Holland. Jacko is now stuffed and on display in the Essex Police Museum.

particular species of crime, and of the habits, haunts and persons of parties known or suspected to live by the commission of crime, also as to prepare themselves for tracing and detecting offenders when any case occurred.

The success of this small branch led to its rapid expansion into the Criminal Investigation Department of Scotland Yard.

The detection of crime relied a great deal upon the guile of individual officers. However, the Victorian era was the age of advancement in the scientific world; it would only be a matter of time before the use of forensic science helped with the detection of crimes and offenders.

One such notable instance was with respect to the poison arsenic. This poison was often referred to as 'inheritance powder' and was used in the commission of many murders. In 1832 a chemist called James Marsh testified in the murder trial of John Bodle. His evidence for the use of arsenic was, in the opinion of the court, flawed and a 'not guilty' verdict was recorded, but Bodle later confessed to the killing. Marsh developed a foolproof test for the presence of arsenic, which involved heating it in a liquid with acid and zinc; when arsenic was present, a metallic deposit was produced. This test was used right up to the 1970s.

Fingerprint technology was introduced to the police service by Henry Faulds (1843–1930). In October 1880 Faulds published a paper on fingerprints. He made two important observations, namely that 'When bloody finger-marks or impressions on clay, glass etc., exist, they may lead to the scientific identification of criminals', and that 'a common

During the late Victorian years technology was advancing at a rapid pace and so revolutionising police work. One notable step was the introduction of photography. The first 'scene of crime' photograph used by the police was of one of the victims of 'Jack the Ripper'. Photographs were also being used to identify and record those persons passing through police custody and those wanted for offences. This camera was used by the Gloucestershire Police for taking such pictures.

As the end of Victoria's reign approached, the use of photography to record criminals developed. This page from an early criminal-records album indicates that the habit of inviting criminals to remove their hats for official photographs had not yet been introduced!

slate or smooth board of any kind, or a sheet of tin, spread over very thinly and evenly with printer's ink, is all that is required to take fingerprints'. In 1886 Faulds offered his fingerprinting system to Scotland Yard, who declined it.

In 1900 a committee was appointed by the Home Secretary to enquire into methods of the 'Identification of Criminals by Measurement and Fingerprints'. About this time, Mr E. R. Henry, later to become Sir Edward Henry, Commissioner of the Metropolitan Police, published his book *The Classification and Use of Fingerprints*. This publication proposed a method of fingerprint classification and comparison to replace the inaccurate Bertillon anthropometric measurement system then in use, which involved skull measurements and only partially relied upon fingerprints for identification. Following the recommendations made by the enquiry committee, the Fingerprint Branch at New Scotland Yard was created in July 1901 using the Henry System of Classification. Faulds died in 1930, having received no recognition for his contribution. It was to be almost another century before a similarly significant advancement was made, with the introduction of deoxyribonucleic acid (DNA) testing.

And so in 1901 this great period of change in the police service passed with the death of Queen Victoria. In the span of one monarch's reign the service had been taken from a medieval system that had been in place for hundreds of years and developed into a revolutionary system of upholding law and order throughout Britain – a system that was the envy of police services throughout the world.

Not everyone was keen to have his photograph taken, as this picture shows. With long time exposures, it is remarkable that anything of a struggling prisoner is recorded at all.

FURTHER READING

Ashley, B. T. *Law and Order.* Batsford, 1967.
Clarke, A. A. *Police Uniform and Equipment.* Shire, 1991.
Critchley, T. A. *A History of Police in England and Wales 900–1966.* Constable, 1967.
Crockford, W. R. *From Cutlasses to Computers: The Police Force in Liverpool 1836–1989.* SB Publications, 1991.
Dumpleton, John. *Law and Order.* A & C Black, 1983.
Fido, Martin, and Skinner, Keith. *The Official Encyclopaedia of Scotland Yard.* Virgin Books, 1999.
Fitzgerald, Percy. *Chronicles of Bow Street Police Office.* Patterson Smith Publishing Corporation, 1972.
Hocking, John. *In the Name of the Law.* Cornish Publications, 1984.
Jones, Owain J. *The History of the Caernarvonshire Constabulary 1856–1950.* Privately published, 1963.
Patrick, John. *Crime and Punishment.* Macmillan Education, 1988.
Reith, C. *A Short History of the British Police.* Oxford University Press, 1948.
Shore, Heather. *Artful Dodgers: Youth and Crime in Early Nineteenth-Century London.* Boydell Press/Royal Historical Society, 1999.
Taylor, David. *The New Police in Nineteenth Century England.* Manchester University Press, 1997.
Taylor, David. *Crime, Policing and Punishment in England 1750–1914.* Macmillan, 1998.
Taylor, M. B., and Wilkinson, V. L. *Badges of Office.* R. Hazell & Company, 1989.
Weinberger, Barbara. *The Best Police in the World: An Oral History of English Policing.* Scholar Press, 1995.
Whitmore, Richard. *Crime and Punishment in Victorian Times.* Batsford, 1978.
Zender, Lucia. *Women, Crime and Custody in Victorian England.* Clarendon Press, 1991.

WEBSITES

www.policehistorysociety.co.uk This site has numerous links to sites with references on policing history, with useful links to other police force sites.
www.devon-cornwall.police.uk Details of all the former constituent forces are given, along with numerous photographs.
www.policehistory.com Both British and international police forces are listed with links to many historical police sites.

PLACES TO VISIT

Many forces other than those mentioned below have museums and archives. However, not all are open to the public and it might be necessary to make an appointment to visit many of them. It is suggested that a telephone call to the respective police force headquarters or the museum office be made to ascertain the public access availability.

Essex Police Museum, Headquarters, Springfield, Chelmsford, Essex CM2 6DA. Telephone: 01245 457150. Website: www.essex.police.uk (By appointment only.)

Fire Police Museum, Peterhouse, 101–109 West Bar, Sheffield, South Yorkshire S3 8PT. Telephone: 0114 249 1999. Website: www.firepolicemuseum.co.uk

Greater Manchester Police Museum, Newton Street, Manchester M1 1ES. Telephone: 0161 856 3287. Website: www.gmp.police.uk (Guided tours available by appointment.)

Kent Police Museum, The Historic Dockyard, Chatham, Kent ME4 4TZ. Telephone: 01634 403260. Website: www.kent-police-museum.co.uk

Metropolitan Police Museum, Unit 7, Meridian Trading Estate, Bugsby's Way, Charlton, London SE7 7SJ. Telephone: 020 8305 2824. Website: www.met.police.co.uk (By appointment only.)

The Police Service of Northern Ireland, Constabulary Headquarters, Brooklyn, Knock Road, Belfast, Northern Ireland BT5 6LE. Telephone: 028 9065 0222. Website: www.psni.police.uk

Porthcawl Museum, The Old Police Station, John Street, Porthcawl, Bridgend, Wales CF36 3BD. Telephone: 01656 782211. Website: www.bridgend.gov.uk

Ripon Police and Prison Museum and Ripon Workhouse, The House of Correction, 27 St Marygate, Ripon, North Yorkshire HG4 1LX. Telephone: 01765 690799. Website: www.riponmuseums.co.uk

Royal Military Police Museum, Defence College of Policing, PPt 38, Southwick Park, Fareham, Hampshire PO17 6EJ. Telephone: 023 9228 4406. Website: www.armymuseums.org.uk

South Wales Police Museum, Police Headquarters, Cowbridge Road, Bridgend, Wales CF31 3SU. Telephone: 01656 303207. Website: www.south-wales.police.uk

Tetbury Police Museum, The Old Court House, 63 Long Street, Tetbury, Gloucestershire GL8 8AA. Telephone: 01666 504670. Website: www.gloucestershire.gov.uk

Thames Valley Police Museum, Thames Valley Police Training Centre, Sulhamstead, near Reading, Berkshire RG7 4DU. Telephone: 0118 932 5748. Website: www.thamesvalley.police.uk (By appointment only.)

Winchcombe Folk and Police Museum, The Town Hall, High Street, Winchcombe GL54 5LJ. Telephone: 01242 609151. Website: www.gloucestershire.gov.uk